Tasty SCHOOL Lunches

Publications International, Ltd.

Favorite Brand Name Recipes at www.fbnr.com

Pictured on the front cover: Stanley Sandwich *(page 11).*

Pictured on the back cover *(left to right):* Chicken Nuggets in a Pocket *(page 8)* and Rabbit Power Brownie Cupcakes *(page 106).*

ISBN-13: 978-1-4127-2678-8
ISBN-10: 1-4127-2678-6

Manufactured in China.

8 7 6 5 4 3 2 1

Microwave Cooking: Microwave ovens vary in wattage. Use the cooking times as guidelines and check for doneness before adding more time.

Preparation/Cooking Times: Preparation times are based on the approximate amount of time required to assemble the recipe before cooking, baking, chilling or serving. These times include preparation steps such as measuring, chopping and mixing. The fact that some preparations and cooking can be done simultaneously is taken into account. Preparation of optional ingredients and serving suggestions is not included.

contents

Tropical Chicken Salad Pockets

3 cups diced cooked chicken*
1 can (20 ounces) pineapple chunks in juice, drained,
    juice reserved
3 green onions, thinly sliced
2 tablespoons chopped fresh cilantro
    Tropical Dressing (recipe follows)
4 pocket breads, split
    Lettuce leaves

**Use home-roasted chicken, or ready-to-eat roasted chicken from the
supermarket or deli.*

In bowl, place chicken, pineapple, green onions, and cilantro.
Pour dressing over chicken mixture and toss to mix. Line each
pocket bread with lettuce leaf; fill with chicken salad.

Makes 4 servings

Tropical Dressing: In small bowl, mix together ½ cup reduced-fat
mayonnaise, 1 tablespoon lime juice, 1 tablespoon reserved
pineapple juice, 1 teaspoon sugar, 1 teaspoon curry powder,
½ teaspoon salt, and ¼ teaspoon grated lime peel. Makes about
⅔ cup dressing.

Favorite recipe from ***Delmarva Poultry Industry, Inc.***

Chicken Nuggets in a Pocket

1 egg
¼ cup milk
1 cup cornbread stuffing, coarsely crushed*
¼ cup grated Parmesan cheese
1 pound boneless skinless chicken breasts, cut into 24 pieces
4 (6-inch) rounds pita bread with pockets, cut crosswise in half
1 cup shredded lettuce
¼ to ½ cup ranch dressing or barbecue sauce

Use seasoned, packaged cornbread stuffing, not croutons.

1. Preheat oven to 400°F. Grease baking sheet; set aside.

2. Beat egg and milk together in shallow bowl. Combine cornbread stuffing and cheese in shallow pan. Dip chicken into egg mixture, then roll chicken in cornbread mixture. Pat nuggets to help cornbread adhere.

3. Place chicken on baking sheet. Bake 8 to 10 minutes or until cooked through and golden.

4. To serve, divide ¼ cup shredded lettuce between pockets of each pita. Add 3 chicken nuggets to each half. Drizzle 1 to 2 tablespoons ranch dressing over each serving.

Makes 4 to 8 servings

Tip

To pack this sandwich for lunch, prepare chicken in advance and chill. Put into the pita bread as directed, wrap and place into insulated lunch bag to keep cool. Spoon ranch dressing into small container and cover tightly. Include a frozen juice box or frozen gel pack. Tell your kids to throw away leftovers.

Travelin' Turkey Subs

3 tablespoons plain yogurt
3 tablespoons ranch salad dressing
1½ cups finely chopped cooked turkey breast
   or smoked turkey breast
½ cup finely chopped broccoli
⅓ cup shredded carrot
4 whole wheat or multi-grain hot dog or
   hamburger buns, split
½ cup (2 ounces) shredded Cheddar cheese
2 tablespoons sunflower seeds or chopped toasted slivered
   almonds (optional)

1. Combine yogurt and salad dressing in medium bowl. Add turkey, broccoli and carrot; mix well.

2. Slightly hollow out tops and bottoms of buns. Sprinkle cheese on bun bottoms. Spoon turkey mixture on top of cheese. Sprinkle with seeds, if desired. Top with bun tops, cut side down. Wrap in plastic wrap. Refrigerate for 2 hours or until thoroughly chilled.

Makes 4 servings

Prep Time: 10 minutes

Quick and Hearty Deli Ham Sub

1 large sandwich roll, sliced in half lengthwise
   Yellow or Dijon mustard, to taste
4 ounces HILLSHIRE FARM® Deli Select Brown Sugar Ham
2 ounces sliced American cheese
⅔ cup cole slaw
   Dill pickle slices, to taste

Spread both cut sides of the roll with mustard to taste.

Fill roll with the remaining ingredients.

Slice in half and serve with your favorite chips.   *Makes 1 serving*

Nutty Albacore Salad Pitas

**1 (3-ounce) STARKIST Flavor Fresh Pouch® Tuna
(Albacore or Chunk Light)**
½ cup mayonnaise
⅓ cup chopped celery
¼ cup raisins or seedless grape halves
¼ cup chopped walnuts, pecans or almonds
½ teaspoon dried dill weed
   Salt and pepper to taste
2 pita breads, halved
4 curly leaf lettuce leaves

In medium bowl, combine tuna, mayonnaise, celery, raisins, nuts
and dill; mix well. Add salt and pepper. Line each pita bread half
with lettuce leaf; fill each with ¼ of tuna mixture.

Makes 4 servings

Prep Time: 10 minutes

Stanley Sandwiches

½ cup shredded carrot
2 tablespoons ranch salad dressing
½ (12-ounce) focaccia bread
3 lettuce leaves
**6 ounces thinly sliced deli-style roast beef, roast chicken
   or roast turkey**

1. Stir together carrot and dressing. Cut focaccia into 3 pieces.
Split each piece horizontally. Place lettuce leaves on bottom
halves. Top with meat. Spoon carrot mixture over meat. Top
with remaining focaccia halves. Wrap in plastic wrap.

2. Pack in insulated bag with ice pack, if desired.

Makes 3 servings

Fantasy Cinnamon Applewiches

4 slices raisin bread
⅓ cup cream cheese, softened
¼ cup finely chopped unpeeled apple
1 teaspoon sugar
⅛ teaspoon ground cinnamon

1. Toast bread. Cut bread into desired shapes using large cookie cutters.

2. Combine cream cheese and apple in small bowl; spread onto toast.

3. Combine sugar and cinnamon in another small bowl; sprinkle evenly over cream cheese mixture.   *Makes 4 servings*

Tip: To pack these sandwiches for lunch, cut 4 additional slices of toasted bread into the same shapes as the bottoms. Top each sandwich with one bread slice. Wrap and refrigerate.

Tuna Schooners

2 (3-ounce) cans water-packed light tuna, drained
½ cup finely chopped apple
¼ cup shredded carrot
⅓ cup ranch salad dressing
4 English muffins, split

1. Combine tuna, apple and carrot in medium bowl. Add salad dressing; mix well.

2. Spread one fourth of tuna mixture over bottom muffin halves. Top with remaining muffin halves. Wrap and refrigerate until ready to pack.   *Makes 4 servings*

Apple and Cheese Pockets

2 medium to large Golden Delicious apples, peeled, cored and finely chopped (2 cups)

2 cups shredded sharp Cheddar cheese

2 tablespoons apple jelly

¼ teaspoon curry powder

1 package (about 16 ounces) refrigerated large biscuits (8 biscuits)

1. Preheat oven to 350°F. Line baking sheet with parchment paper; set aside.

2. Combine apples, cheese, apple jelly and curry powder in large bowl; mix well.

3. Roll out each biscuit on lightly floured board to 6½-inch circle. Place ½ cup apple mixture in center. Fold biscuit over filling to form a semicircle, and press to seal tightly. Place on baking sheet. Bake 15 to 18 minutes or until biscuits are golden and filling is hot.

4. To keep hot for lunch, place in vacuum container and close. Or, reheat pockets in microwave, if available, about 30 seconds on HIGH until hot.

Makes 8 servings

Tip

When packing hot foods such as soups, pastas and hot sandwiches, preheat a vacuum container with boiling water. Dry and fill with piping hot food. To keep food hot, be sure your child doesn't open the thermos before lunchtime.

Tasty **SCHOOL** Lunches

Sub on the Run

  2 hard rolls (2 ounces each), split into halves
  4 tomato slices
 14 turkey pepperoni slices
  2 ounces oven-roasted turkey breast
 ¼ cup (1 ounce) shredded mozzarella or sharp Cheddar cheese
  1 cup packaged coleslaw mix or shredded lettuce
 ¼ medium green bell pepper, thinly sliced (optional)
  2 tablespoons prepared Italian salad dressing

1. Top bottom halves of rolls with 2 tomato slices, 7 pepperoni slices, half of turkey, 2 tablespoons cheese, ½ cup coleslaw mix and half of bell pepper slices, if desired.

2. Drizzle with salad dressing. Top with roll tops.

Makes 2 servings

Peanut Pitas

  1 package (8 ounces) small rounds pita bread, cut
     crosswise in half
 16 teaspoons peanut butter
 16 teaspoons strawberry spreadable fruit
  1 large banana, peeled and thinly sliced (about 48 slices)

1. Spread inside of each pita half with 1 teaspoon each peanut butter and spreadable fruit.

2. Fill pita halves evenly with banana slices.   *Makes 8 servings*

Honey Bees: Substitute honey for spreadable fruit.

Jolly Jellies: Substitute any flavor jelly for spreadable fruit and thin apple slices for banana slices.

Crunchy Turkey Pita Pockets

1 cup diced cooked turkey breast or chicken breast
½ cup packaged coleslaw mix
½ cup dried cranberries
¼ cup shredded carrots
2 tablespoons mayonnaise
1 tablespoon honey mustard
2 (6-inch) rounds whole wheat pita bread

1. Combine turkey, coleslaw mix, cranberries, carrots, mayonnaise and mustard in small bowl; mix well.

2. Cut pitas crosswise in half; fill with turkey mixture.

Makes 2 to 4 servings

Best Ever Beef Heroes

3 tablespoons mayonnaise
1 tablespoon Dijon mustard
2 teaspoons prepared horseradish
4 submarine or hoagie rolls, split
4 red leaf or romaine lettuce leaves
1 pound sliced deli roast beef
1 thin slice red onion, separated into rings
8 slices SARGENTO® Deli Style Sliced Swiss Cheese

1. Combine mayonnaise, mustard and horseradish; mix well. Spread on cut sides of rolls.

2. Fill rolls with lettuce, roast beef, onion rings and cheese. Close sandwiches; cut in half.

Makes 4 servings

Prep Time: 10 minutes

Peanut Butter
and Fruit Pita Pockets

1 large crisp apple, peeled, cored and finely diced
1 medium Bartlett pear, peeled, cored and finely diced
1½ teaspoons raisins
2 teaspoons orange juice
3 tablespoons super chunk peanut butter
4 large lettuce leaves or 8 large spinach leaves
2 whole wheat pitas, about 2 ounces each

1. Combine diced apples, pears and raisins with orange juice and hold for 5 minutes. Add peanut butter and mix well.

2. Wash and dry lettuce or spinach leaves on absorbent paper towels. Tear lettuce into pita size pieces.

3. Warm pita in toaster on lowest color setting. Cut pita in half, and carefully open each half to make a pocket.

4. Line each pocket with lettuce or spinach leaves and spoon in equal portions of fruit and peanut butter mixture. Serve and enjoy. *Makes 2 to 4 servings*

Note: A delicious and fun snack kids of all ages can make and enjoy...Sh-h-h-h, it's super healthy!

Favorite recipe from *Chilean Fresh Fruit Association*

Tip

To prevent sandwiches from getting soggy, pack the filling and bread in separate containers. Include a plastic spoon in the lunch bag so kids can put the filling in the bread just before eating.

Stacked Kaisers with Sweet Spiced Spread

⅓ cup mayonnaise
¼ cup prepared yellow mustard
1 tablespoon packed dark brown sugar
1 teaspoon prepared horseradish
⅛ teaspoon ground cinnamon
4 kaiser rolls, split into halves
6 ounces thinly sliced deli honey baked ham
6 ounces thinly sliced deli smoked turkey
3 ounces sliced Swiss cheese
3 ounces sliced American cheese
3 ounces (½ cup) thinly sliced green bell pepper
1 ounce (¼ cup) thinly sliced red onion

1. In a small bowl, combine mayonnaise, mustard, sugar, horseradish and cinnamon. Stir until well blended.

2. Coat cut sides of each roll with about 1 tablespoon mayonnaise mixture.

3. Place equal amounts of the ham, turkey, Swiss and American cheeses, bell pepper and onion on roll bottoms. Top with the remaining roll tops. Press down gently. *Makes 4 to 8 servings*

Tip

To help keep perishable foods at the proper temperature for food safety, thoroughly chill all ingredients. Prepare and individually wrap food items. Then, refrigerate up to 2 hours or overnight before packing.

Dem Bones

1 package (6 ounces) sliced ham
¾ cup (3 ounces) shredded Swiss cheese
½ cup mayonnaise
1 tablespoon sweet pickle relish
½ teaspoon yellow mustard
¼ teaspoon black pepper
6 slices white bread

1. Place ham in bowl of food processor or blender; process until ground. Place ham, cheese, mayonnaise, relish, mustard and pepper in small bowl; mix well.

2. Cut out 12 bone shapes from bread using 3½-inch bone-shaped cookie cutter. Spread half of "bones" with 2 tablespoons ham mixture; top with remaining "bones."   *Makes 3 to 6 servings*

Ranch Bacon and Egg Salad Sandwich

6 hard-cooked eggs, cooled and peeled
¼ cup HIDDEN VALLEY® The Original Ranch® Dressing
¼ cup diced celery
3 tablespoons crisp-cooked, crumbled bacon*
1 tablespoon diced green onion
8 slices sandwich bread
  Lettuce and tomato (optional)

*Bacon pieces can be used.

Coarsely chop eggs. Combine with dressing, celery, bacon and onion in a medium mixing bowl; mix well. Chill until just before serving. Spread salad evenly on 4 bread slices; arrange lettuce and tomato on egg salad, if desired. Top with remaining bread slices.
                    Makes 4 servings

Tuna Salad Pita Pockets

1 can (9 ounces) tuna, drained
1 cup chopped cucumber
¼ cup ricotta cheese
2 tablespoons mayonnaise
2 tablespoons red wine vinegar
2 green onions, chopped
1 tablespoon sweet pickle relish
2 cloves garlic, finely chopped
½ teaspoon salt
¼ teaspoon black pepper
1 cup alfalfa sprouts
2 rounds pita bread, cut crosswise in half

Combine all ingredients except sprouts and bread. Equally divide sprouts and tuna mixture among pita pockets.

Makes 4 servings

Tip

To help keep cold foods
at right temperature for food safety,
pack food in insulated bags. Also,
keep gel packs in the freezer so they
are ready to pop in a lunch bag at
the last minute.

Tasty
SCHOOL
Lunches

Apricot Chicken Sandwiches

**6 ounces cooked chicken tenders *or* 1 package (about
6 ounces) refrigerated fully cooked chicken breast strips***
2 tablespoons apricot fruit spread
2 tablespoons chopped fresh apricots (pits removed)
4 slices whole wheat bread
4 lettuce leaves

**Fully cooked chicken breast strips can be found in the prepared meats section
of the meat case.*

1. Chop chicken. Place chicken, apricot spread and apricots in
small bowl; mix well.

2. Top 2 slices bread with lettuce leaves. Divide chicken mixture
evenly between bread slices. Top with remaining bread slices. Cut
each sandwich into fourths making 4 wedges.

Makes 2 to 4 servings

Tip

Add variety to school lunches
with foods that are healthy and easy
to pack, such as graham crackers, mini
rice cakes, bread sticks, grapes, cheese
cubes, pretzels, vanilla wafers, yogurt
raisins, string cheese sticks and
dried fruit.

Rock 'n' Rollers

  4 (6- to 7-inch) flour tortillas
  4 ounces Neufchâtel cheese, softened
  ⅓ cup peach preserves
  1 cup (4 ounces) shredded Cheddar cheese
  ½ cup packed, stemmed and washed fresh spinach leaves
  3 ounces thinly sliced regular or smoked turkey breast

1. Spread each tortilla evenly with 1 ounce Neufchâtel cheese; cover with thin layer of preserves. Sprinkle with Cheddar cheese.

2. Arrange spinach leaves and turkey over Cheddar cheese. Roll up tortillas; trim ends. Cover and refrigerate until ready to serve.

3. Cut "rollers" crosswise in half or diagonally into 1-inch pieces.

Makes 4 servings

Sassy Salsa Rollers: Substitute salsa for peach preserves and shredded iceberg lettuce for spinach leaves.

Ham 'n' Apple Rollers: Omit peach preserves and spinach leaves. Substitute lean ham slices for turkey. Spread tortillas with Neufchâtel cheese as directed; sprinkle with Cheddar cheese. Top each tortilla with about 2 tablespoons finely chopped apple and 2 ham slices; roll up. Continue as directed.

Wedgies: Prepare Rock 'n' Rollers or any variation as directed, but do not roll up. Top with second tortilla; cut into wedges.

Peanut Butter-Apple Wraps

¾ **cup creamy peanut butter**
4 **(7-inch) whole wheat or spinach tortillas or 8-grain lavash**
¾ **cup finely chopped apple**
⅓ **cup shredded carrot**
⅓ **cup granola without raisins**
1 **tablespoon toasted wheat germ**

Spread peanut butter evenly on one side of each tortilla. Sprinkle each tortilla evenly with apple, carrot, granola and wheat germ. Roll up tightly. Refrigerate until ready to pack.

Makes 4 servings

Light & Tasty Tuna Salad Wrapwich

HELLMANN'S® or BEST FOODS® Light Mayonnaise or Just 2 Good!® Mayonnaise Dressing
4 **(10-inch) flavored flour tortillas**
  Arugula or torn red leaf lettuce leaves
½ **cup thinly sliced cucumber**
1 **cup chopped tomato**
¾ **cup chopped red onion**
2 **cans (6½ ounces each) solid white tuna packed in water, drained and flaked**

1. Spread It: Spread Hellmann's or Best Foods Light Mayonnaise or Just 2 Good! Mayonnaise Dressing onto tortillas.

2. Stuff It: Layer arugula, cucumber, tomato and red onion down center of each tortilla. Top with tuna and season, if desired, with salt and ground black pepper.

3. Wrap It: Roll & fold the filled tortilla & pop it into a WrapWich wrapper. Or, make one yourself out of aluminum foil or waxed paper.

Makes 4 to 8 servings

Prep Time: 15 minutes

Peanut Butter-Apple Wraps

Sassy Southwestern Veggie Wraps

½ cup diced zucchini
½ cup diced red or yellow bell pepper
½ cup frozen corn, thawed and drained
1 jalapeño pepper,* seeded and chopped (optional)
¾ cup (3 ounces) shredded Mexican cheese blend
3 tablespoons prepared salsa or picante sauce
2 (8-inch) flour tortillas

*Jalapeño peppers can sting and irritate the skin, so wear rubber gloves when handling peppers and do not touch your eyes.

1. Combine zucchini, bell pepper, corn and jalapeño pepper, if desired, in small bowl. Stir in cheese and salsa; mix well.

2. Soften tortillas according to package directions. Spoon vegetable mixture down center of tortillas, distributing evenly; roll up burrito-style. Serve wraps cold or warm.**

Makes 2 servings

**To warm each wrap, cover loosely with plastic wrap and microwave on HIGH 40 to 45 seconds or until cheese is melted.

Smoked Turkey Tortilla Roll-Ups

4 (10-inch) flour tortillas
4 tablespoons *French's*® Sweet & Tangy Honey Mustard
½ pound sliced smoked turkey or ham
1 cup shredded lettuce
1 cup chopped tomatoes

1. Spread each flour tortilla with *1 tablespoon* mustard. Top with 2 slices turkey and ¼ cup *each* lettuce and tomatoes.

2. Roll up jelly-roll style. Wrap in plastic wrap; chill. Cut in half to serve.

Makes 4 servings

Prep Time: 10 minutes

Sassy Southwestern Veggie Wrap

Inside-Out Breadsticks

1 package (about 11 ounces) refrigerated breadsticks (12 breadsticks)
1 package (8 ounces) cream cheese, softened
1 to 2 tablespoons milk
¼ cup finely chopped carrots
2 tablespoons minced chives or green onion, green part only
12 slices deli ham, roast beef, turkey or chicken

1. Bake breadsticks according to package directions; cool.

2. Beat together cream cheese and enough milk for spreading consistency. Stir in carrots and chives. Spread 1 rounded tablespoon cream cheese mixture over ham slice. Roll ham slice around breadstick. Wrap in plastic wrap to seal. Refrigerate until ready to pack in lunchbox. *Makes 6 to 12 servings*

Serving Suggestion: Use the cream cheese spread as a dip for broccoli spears or celery sticks. For dipping consistency, thin the cream cheese with 1 to 2 additional tablespoons milk, then pack in small container with tight-fitting lid.

Tip

Resealable food storage bags are lunch lifesavers. They conveniently hold and protect portioned food items. When using plastic bags, blow air into the bag before closing. The air will cushion the food and keep it from getting smashed.

Cinnamon-Raisin Roll-Ups

4 ounces cream cheese, softened
½ cup shredded carrot
¼ cup golden or dark raisins
1 tablespoon honey
¼ teaspoon ground cinnamon
4 (7- to 8-inch) whole wheat or regular flour tortillas
8 thin apple wedges

1. Combine cream cheese, carrot, raisins, honey and cinnamon in small bowl; mix well.

2. Spread tortillas evenly with cream cheese mixture, leaving ½-inch border around edge of each tortilla. Place 2 apple wedges down center of each tortilla; roll up. Wrap in plastic wrap. Refrigerate until ready to serve. *Makes 4 servings*

Tip: For extra convenience, prepare roll-ups the night before. In the morning, pack roll-up in lunch box along with a frozen juice box. The juice box will be thawed by lunchtime and will keep the snack cold in the meantime!

Ham Tortillas with Picante Sauce

2 tablespoons mayonnaise or salad dressing
1 tablespoon picante sauce
2 (8-inch) flour tortillas
4 thin slices CURE 81® ham
Shredded lettuce
Chopped tomato

In small bowl, combine mayonnaise and picante sauce. Spread tortillas with mayonnaise mixture. Top each tortilla with two ham slices, lettuce and tomato. Roll up. Serve with additional picante sauce, if desired. *Makes 2 servings*

Inside-Out Turkey Sandwiches

2 tablespoons cream cheese
2 tablespoons pasteurized process cheese spread
2 teaspoons chopped green onion tops
1 teaspoon prepared mustard
12 thin round slices turkey breast or smoked turkey breast
4 large pretzel logs or unsalted breadsticks

1. Combine cream cheese, process cheese spread, green onion and mustard in small bowl; mix well.

2. Arrange 3 turkey slices on large sheet of plastic wrap, overlapping slices in center. Spread ¼ of cream cheese mixture evenly onto turkey slices, covering slices completely. Place 1 pretzel at bottom edge of turkey slices; roll up turkey around pretzel. (Be sure to keep all 3 turkey slices together as you roll them around pretzel.)

3. Repeat with remaining ingredients. *Makes 4 servings*

PB & J Sandwich

2 slices sandwich bread
2 tablespoons peanut butter
Favorite Toppings (recipe follows)

1. Spread peanut butter on 1 slice bread.

2. Top with one or more favorite toppings. Close sandwich with bread slice. Cut into 4 wedges. *Makes 1 to 2 servings*

Favorite Toppings: ½ sliced banana, 1 tablespoon strawberry jam or grape jelly, ¼ cup sliced strawberries, 1 small sliced apple, 2 tablespoons raisins, 2 tablespoons grated carrot, 2 slices crumbled crisp-cooked bacon or 1 tablespoon chopped nuts.

Rainbow Spirals

4 (10-inch) flour tortillas (assorted flavors and colors)
4 tablespoons *French's*® Mustard (any flavor)
½ pound (about 8 slices) thinly sliced deli roast beef,
      bologna or turkey
8 slices American, provolone or Muenster cheese
      Fancy party toothpicks

1. Spread each tortilla with *1 tablespoon* mustard. Layer with meat and cheeses dividing evenly.

2. Roll up jelly-roll style; secure with toothpicks and cut into thirds.   *Makes 4 to 6 servings*

Prep Time: 10 minutes

California Beach Club Wrap

½ cup garden vegetable-flavored cream cheese
4 (10-inch) flour tortillas
¼ pound JENNIE-O TURKEY STORE® Turkey, thinly sliced
¼ pound CURE 81® Ham, thinly sliced
4 (1-ounce) American cheese slices
2 Roma tomatoes thinly sliced
¼ cup HORMEL® Real Bacon Bits or pieces
1 avocado, peeled and diced

Spread cream cheese to within ½ inch of edge of each tortilla. Layer each tortilla with ¼ of turkey and ham. Top with cheese slices, sliced tomatoes, bacon pieces and diced avocado. Roll up tortillas. Slice diagonally in half and serve.   *Makes 4 servings*

Prep Time: 30 minutes

Backbones

4 extra-large flour tortillas
1 package (3½ ounces) soft cheese spread with herbs
1 bag (6 ounces) fresh baby spinach
8 ounces thinly sliced salami or ham
8 ounces thinly sliced Havarti or Swiss cheese
1 jar (7 ounces) roasted red bell peppers, drained and sliced into thin strips

1. For each tortilla, spread 2 to 3 tablespoons cheese all the way to edge. Layer evenly with one fourth of spinach, meat and cheese. Place red bell pepper strips down center. Tightly roll up; slice off and discard rounded ends. Repeat with remaining tortillas and filling ingredients.

2. Cut tortilla rolls into 1½-inch slices, if desired.

Makes 4 to 8 servings

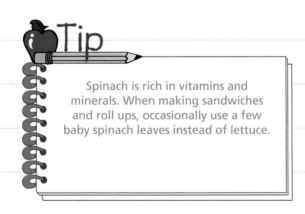

Tip

Spinach is rich in vitamins and minerals. When making sandwiches and roll ups, occasionally use a few baby spinach leaves instead of lettuce.

Pizza Dippin' Strips

1 package (13.8 ounces) refrigerated pizza crust dough
15 thin slices pepperoni
1 cup shredded mozzarella cheese (about 4 ounces)
1 jar (1 pound 10 ounces) RAGÚ® Organic Pasta Sauce

Preheat oven to 400°.

On greased baking sheet, roll pizza dough into 12×9-inch rectangle. Fold edges over to make ¾-inch crust. Bake 7 minutes.

Evenly top pizza crust with pepperoni, then cheese. Bake an additional 8 minutes or until cheese is melted. Let stand 2 minutes.

Cut pizza in half lengthwise, then into 1½-inch strips. Serve with Pasta Sauce for dipping.   *Makes 16 strips*

Prep Time: 10 minutes • **Cook Time:** 15 minutes

Kids' Wraps

4 teaspoons Dijon honey mustard
2 (8-inch) flour tortillas
2 slices American cheese, cut in half
4 ounces thinly sliced oven-roasted turkey breast
½ cup shredded carrot (about 1 medium)
3 romaine lettuce leaves, washed and torn into bite-size pieces

1. Spread 2 teaspoons mustard evenly over 1 tortilla.

2. Top with 2 cheese halves, half of turkey, half of shredded carrot and half of torn lettuce.

3. Roll up tortilla; cut in half. Repeat with remaining ingredients.
Makes 2 servings

Sammich Swirls

1 package (11-ounce can) refrigerated French bread dough
Seasoning mix (optional)
Yellow mustard (optional)
4 slices bologna
4 slices provolone cheese
2 teaspoons grated Parmesan cheese

1. Preheat oven to 350°F. Roll out bread dough to 10×12-inch rectangle. If desired, sprinkle with seasoning mix and dot with mustard.

2. Arrange bologna and cheese in alternating circles, overlapping edges to cover dough. Roll up lengthwise like a jelly roll; pinch seams shut. Place dough, seam side down, on baking sheet. Sprinkle with grated Parmesan cheese.

3. Bake 25 to 30 minutes or until puffy and browned. Let cool. Cut into 1-inch-thick portions. *Makes 4 servings*

Pizza Rollers

1 package (10 ounces) refrigerated pizza dough
½ cup pizza sauce
18 slices turkey pepperoni
6 sticks mozzarella cheese

1. Preheat oven to 425°F. Coat baking sheet with nonstick cooking spray.

2. Roll out pizza dough on baking sheet to form 12×9-inch rectangle. Cut pizza dough into 6 (4½×4-inch) rectangles. Spread about 1 tablespoon sauce over center third of each rectangle. Top with 3 slices pepperoni and stick of mozzarella cheese. Bring ends of dough together over cheese, pinching to seal. Place seam side down on prepared baking sheet.

3. Bake in center of oven 10 minutes or until golden brown.
Makes 6 servings

Kids' Quesadillas

8 slices American cheese
8 (10-inch) flour tortillas
½ pound thinly sliced deli turkey
6 tablespoons *French's*® **Sweet & Tangy Honey Mustard**
2 tablespoons melted butter
¼ teaspoon paprika

1. To prepare 1 quesadilla, arrange 2 slices of cheese on 1 tortilla. Top with ¼ of the turkey. Spread with *1½ tablespoons* mustard, then top with another tortilla. Prepare 3 more quesadillas with remaining ingredients.

2. Combine butter and paprika. Brush one side of tortilla with butter mixture. Preheat 12-inch nonstick skillet over medium-high heat. Arrange tortilla butter side down and cook 2 minutes. Brush top of tortilla with butter mixture and turn over. Cook 1½ minutes or until golden brown. Repeat with remaining 3 quesadillas.

3. Cool and slice into wedges.   *Makes 4 servings*

Prep Time: 5 minutes • **Cook Time:** 15 minutes

Tip

Whether you use a brown bag, lunchbox or insulated bag, find a container that is appropriate for the age of your child and the type of food being packed. Younger children like fancy containers while teens want completely disposable brown bags.

Kids' Quesadillas

Tasty Tortellini Salad

8 ounces refrigerated cheese-filled tortellini
    or cheese-filled cappelletti
1½ cups broccoli florets
  1 cup sliced carrots
⅔ cup creamy Caesar salad dressing
½ cup grape tomatoes, halved
  2 tablespoons sliced green onion
  3 tablespoons toasted soy nuts or sunflower seeds (optional)

1. Cook pasta according to package directions; drain. Rinse with cold water; drain well.

2. Combine pasta, broccoli, carrots, salad dressing, tomatoes and green onion in large bowl. Gently toss. Cover and refrigerate 2 hours or until well chilled. Sprinkle with seeds.

Makes 3 to 6 servings

Variation: Substitute any type of vegetables such as diced zucchini or diced bell peppers for broccoli or carrots in pasta salad. Eating small bites of vegetables with pasta is a great way to introduce new tastes. Or, let your kids pick up veggies from the salad bar such as peas or edamame to add to pasta salad. You might be surprised by what they will eat.

Prep Time: 15 minutes • **Chill Time:** 2 hours

Italian Vegetable Soup

1 tablespoon olive oil
1 cup finely chopped red onion (1 medium onion)
1 cup chopped red bell pepper (1 medium pepper)
3 cans (about 14 ounces each) chicken broth
1 bag (16 ounces) frozen Italian vegetables
    or mixed vegetables
1 can (about 15 ounces) chickpeas, rinsed and drained
1 can (about 14 ounces) diced tomatoes
½ teaspoon salt
½ teaspoon black pepper
⅛ teaspoon dried oregano
1 cup uncooked wagon wheel pasta
1 cup cooked diced chicken (optional)

1. Heat oil in Dutch oven. Add onion and bell pepper. Cook and stir over medium-high heat 3 minutes or until onion is tender. Stir in chicken broth, frozen vegetables, chickpeas, tomatoes, salt, pepper and oregano. Bring to a boil over high heat.

2. Stir in pasta and chicken, if desired. Reduce heat to low; cook 15 minutes or until pasta is tender. *Makes 6 servings*

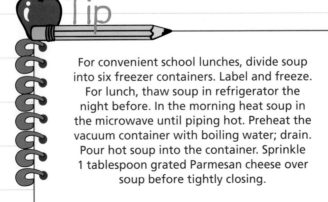

Tip

For convenient school lunches, divide soup into six freezer containers. Label and freeze. For lunch, thaw soup in refrigerator the night before. In the morning heat soup in the microwave until piping hot. Preheat the vacuum container with boiling water; drain. Pour hot soup into the container. Sprinkle 1 tablespoon grated Parmesan cheese over soup before tightly closing.

A-B-C Minestrone

1 tablespoon olive oil
1 medium onion, chopped
2 medium carrots, chopped
1 small zucchini, chopped
½ teaspoon dried Italian seasoning
4 cups chicken broth
1 jar (1 pound 10 ounces) RAGÚ® OLD WORLD STYLE®
  Pasta Sauce
1 can (15.5 ounces) cannellini or white kidney beans,
  rinsed and drained
1 cup alphabet pasta

In 4-quart saucepan, heat olive oil over medium heat and cook onion, carrots and zucchini, stirring frequently, 5 minutes or until vegetables are tender. Add Italian seasoning and cook, stirring occasionally, 1 minute. Add broth and Pasta Sauce and bring to a boil. Stir in beans and pasta. Cook, stirring occasionally, 10 minutes or until pasta is tender.

Serve, if desired, with chopped parsley and grated Parmesan cheese.   *Makes 8 servings*

Prep Time: 10 minutes • **Cook Time:** 20 minutes

Tip

Crunchy toppings such as oyster crackers, goldfish crackers, crispy croutons and tortilla chips add fun and flavor to soups. Pack a small bag of your child's favorite topping to go with a thermos of soup.

Cheesy Flower Power Pasta Bake

1 jar (1 pound 10 ounces) RAGÚ® Organic Pasta Sauce
1½ cups water
1 container (15 ounces) ricotta cheese
2 cups shredded mozzarella cheese (about 8 ounces)
¼ cup grated Parmesan cheese
8 ounces flower-shaped (fiori) pasta

Preheat oven to 400°.

In large bowl, combine Pasta Sauce and water. Stir in ricotta, 1 cup mozzarella and Parmesan cheese, then uncooked pasta.

In 13×9-inch baking dish, evenly spoon pasta mixture. Cover tightly with aluminum foil and bake 45 minutes.

Remove foil, then sprinkle with remaining 1 cup mozzarella cheese. Bake, uncovered, an additional 5 minutes or until mozzarella is melted. Let stand 10 minutes before serving.   *Makes 8 servings*

Prep Time: 10 minutes • **Cook Time:** 50 minutes

Rainbow Pasta

Water
2 teaspoons salt
1 teaspoon each green, red, blue and yellow food colorings
1 box (16 ounces) your favorite shaped pasta
1 jar (1 pound) RAGÚ® Cheesy! Classic Alfredo Sauce, heated

In each of four 2- or 3-quart saucepans, bring 6 cups water and ½ teaspoon salt to a boil over high heat. Stir 1 teaspoon food coloring and ¼ pound pasta into each saucepan. Cook according to package directions; drain and rinse.

Toss colored pastas together and serve with Alfredo Sauce.

Makes 8 servings

Prep Time: 5 minutes • **Cook Time:** 20 minutes

Mexican Turkey
Chili Mac

1 pound ground turkey
1 package (1¼ ounces) reduced-sodium taco seasoning mix
1 can (14½ ounces) reduced-sodium stewed tomatoes
1 can (11 ounces) corn with red and green peppers, undrained
1½ cups cooked elbow macaroni, without salt, drained
1 ounce low-salt corn chips, crushed
½ cup shredded reduced-fat Cheddar cheese

1. In large nonstick skillet, over medium-high heat, sauté turkey 5 to 6 minutes or until no longer pink; drain. Stir in taco seasoning, tomatoes, corn and macaroni. Reduce heat to medium and cook 4 to 5 minutes until heated throughout.

2. Sprinkle corn chips over meat mixture and top with cheese. Cover and heat 1 to 2 minutes or until cheese is melted.

Makes 6 servings

Favorite recipe from **National Turkey Federation**

Pizza Soup

2 cans (10¾ ounces each) condensed tomato soup
¾ teaspoon garlic powder
½ teaspoon dried oregano leaves
¾ cup uncooked tiny pasta shells (¼-inch)
1 cup shredded quick-melting mozzarella cheese
1 cup *French's*® French Fried Onions

1. Combine soup, *2 soup cans of water,* garlic powder and oregano in small saucepan. Bring to boiling over medium-high heat.

2. Add pasta. Cook 8 minutes or until pasta is tender.

3. Stir in cheese. Cook until cheese melts. Sprinkle with French Fried Onions.

Makes 4 servings

Prep Time: 5 minutes • **Cook Time:** 10 minutes

Macaroni and Cheese Pronto

8 ounces uncooked elbow macaroni
1 can (10¾ ounces) cream of Cheddar cheese soup, undiluted
½ cup milk
2 cups diced cooked ham (about ½ pound)
1 cup (4 ounces) shredded Cheddar cheese
½ cup frozen green peas
Black pepper

1. Cook macaroni according to package directions. Drain and set aside.

2. Meanwhile, combine soup and milk in medium saucepan. Cook and stir over medium heat until smooth.

3. Add ham, cheese, peas and cooked macaroni to soup mixture. Reduce heat to low; cook and stir 5 minutes or until cheese melts and mixture is heated through. Add pepper to taste.

Makes 4 servings

Prep and Cook Time: 20 minutes

Tip

Perfectly cooked pasta should be al dente—tender but still firm to the bite. Test pasta shortly before the time recommended on the package to avoid overcooking.

Silly Spaghetti Casserole

8 ounces uncooked spaghetti, broken in half
¼ cup finely grated Parmesan cheese
¼ cup cholesterol-free egg substitute *or* 1 egg
¾ pound ground turkey or ground beef
⅓ cup chopped onion
2 cups pasta sauce
½ (10-ounce) package frozen cut spinach, thawed and squeezed dry
¾ cup (3 ounces) shredded mozzarella cheese
1 green or yellow bell pepper, cored and seeded

1. Preheat oven to 350°F. Spray 8-inch square baking dish with nonstick cooking spray.

2. Cook spaghetti according to package directions; drain.

3. Return spaghetti to saucepan. Add Parmesan cheese and egg substitute; toss. Place in prepared baking dish.

4. Spray large nonstick skillet with cooking spray. Cook turkey and onion in skillet over medium-high heat until meat is lightly browned, stirring to break up meat. Drain fat. Stir in pasta sauce and spinach. Spoon on top of spaghetti mixture.

5. Sprinkle with mozzarella cheese. Use small cookie cutter to cut decorative shapes from bell pepper. Arrange on top of cheese.

6. Cover with foil. Bake 40 to 45 minutes or until bubbling. Let stand 10 minutes. Cut into squares.　　*Makes 6 servings*

Ragú® Burrito Bake

1 pound lean ground beef or ground turkey

2 cups diced fresh vegetables*

4½ teaspoons chili powder

1 can (15.25 ounces) whole kernel corn, drained

1 jar (1 pound 10 ounces) RAGÚ® OLD WORLD STYLE® Pasta Sauce

6 (8½ inches) regular or whole wheat flour tortillas

2 cups shredded cheddar cheese or low fat cheddar cheese (about 8 ounces)

Use any combination of the following: red bell pepper, yellow squash, zucchini and onion.

Preheat oven to 350°F. In 12-inch nonstick skillet, brown ground beef over medium-high heat, drain if desired. Stir in vegetables and chili powder and cook 5 minutes or until vegetables are softened. Stir in corn and 1 cup Pasta Sauce. Simmer, uncovered, 1 minute; remove from heat.

In 13×9-inch baking dish, spread 1 cup remaining Pasta Sauce; set aside. Evenly fill tortillas with ground beef mixture and 1 cup cheese; roll up and place seam-side down in prepared dish. Top tortillas with remaining Pasta Sauce.

Bake 30 minutes. Top with remaining cheese and bake an additional 10 minutes or until sauce is bubbling and cheese is melted.   *Makes 6 servings*

Prep Time: 10 minutes • **Cook Time:** 40 minutes

Quick Taco
Macaroni & Cheese

**1 package (12 ounces) large elbow macaroni (4 cups dried
    pasta)**
1 tablespoon LAWRY'S® Seasoned Salt
1 pound lean ground beef or turkey
1 package (1 ounce) LAWRY'S® Taco Spices & Seasonings
2 cups (8 ounces) shredded Colby longhorn cheese
2 cups (8 ounces) shredded mild cheddar cheese
2 cups milk
3 eggs, beaten

In large stockpot, boil macaroni in unsalted water just until tender.
Drain and toss with Seasoned Salt. Meanwhile in medium skillet,
brown ground meat; drain fat. Stir in Taco Spices & Seasonings.
Spray 13×9×2-inch baking dish with nonstick cooking spray. Layer
half of macaroni in bottom of dish. Top with half of cheeses.
Spread taco meat over top and repeat layers of macaroni and
cheeses. In medium bowl, beat together milk and eggs. Pour egg
mixture over top of casserole. Bake in preheated 350°F oven for
30 to 35 minutes or until golden brown.   *Makes 6 to 8 servings*

Variation: For spicier flavor, try using LAWRY'S® Chili Spices
& Seasonings or LAWRY'S® Hot Taco Spices & Seasonings instead
of Taco Spices & Seasonings.

Prep Time: 20 to 22 minutes • Cook Time: 30 to 35 minutes

Pizza Meatball and Noodle Soup

1 can (14 ounces) beef broth
½ cup chopped onion
½ cup chopped carrot
**2 ounces uncooked whole wheat spaghetti,
    broken into 2- to 3-inch pieces**
1 cup zucchini slices, cut in half
8 ounces frozen fully-cooked Italian-style meatballs
1 can (8 ounces) pizza sauce

1. Combine broth, onion and carrot in large saucepan. Add spaghetti. Bring to a boil. Reduce heat; simmer, covered, 3 minutes.

2. Add zucchini, meatballs and pizza sauce to broth mixture. Return to a boil. Reduce heat. Simmer, covered, 8 to 9 minutes more or until meatballs are hot and spaghetti is tender, stirring frequently.

Makes 4 servings

Prep Time: 15 minutes

Hot Diggity Dots & Twisters

⅔ cup milk
2 tablespoons margarine or butter
**1 (4.8-ounce) package PASTA RONI® Four Cheese Flavor
    with Corkscrew Pasta**
1½ cups frozen peas
4 hot dogs, cut into ½-inch pieces
2 teaspoons mustard

1. In large saucepan, bring 1¼ cups water, milk and margarine just to a boil.

2. Stir in pasta, peas and Special Seasonings; return to a boil. Reduce heat to medium. Gently boil uncovered, 7 to 8 minutes or until pasta is tender, stirring occasionally.

3. Stir in hot dogs and mustard. Let stand 3 to 5 minutes before serving.

Makes 4 servings

Prep Time: 5 minutes • **Cook Time:** 15 minutes

Feelin' Good Vegetable Soup

½ **pound ground turkey or ground beef**
1 **can (about 14 ounces) chicken or beef broth**
1 **can (8 ounces) tomato sauce**
½ **cup uncooked small shell pasta**
1 **teaspoon chili powder or Cajun seasoning**
½ **teaspoon dried basil**
⅛ **teaspoon garlic powder**
1½ **cups frozen mixed vegetables**

1. Brown turkey in medium saucepan over medium-high heat, stirring to break up meat; drain fat. Stir in broth, tomato sauce, pasta, chili powder, basil and garlic powder. Bring to a boil. Reduce heat; simmer, covered, 5 minutes.

2. Stir in vegetables. Bring to a boil. Simmer, covered, 5 minutes or until pasta is tender. *Makes 4 servings*

Prep Time: 15 minutes

Quick & Easy Meatball Soup

1 **package (15 to 18 ounces) frozen Italian sausage meatballs without sauce**
2 **cans (about 14 ounces each) Italian-style stewed tomatoes**
2 **cans (about 14 ounces each) beef broth**
1 **can (about 14 ounces) mixed vegetables**
½ **cup uncooked rotini pasta or small macaroni**
½ **teaspoon dried oregano**

1. Thaw meatballs in microwave oven according to package directions.

2. Place remaining ingredients in large saucepan. Add meatballs. Bring to a boil. Reduce heat; cover and simmer 15 minutes or until pasta is tender. *Makes 4 to 6 servings*

Kid's Choice
Meatballs

1½ pounds ground beef
¼ cup dry seasoned bread crumbs
¼ cup grated Parmesan cheese
3 tablespoons *French's*® Worcestershire Sauce
1 egg
2 jars (14 ounces each) spaghetti sauce

1. Preheat oven to 425°F. In bowl, gently mix beef, bread crumbs, cheese, Worcestershire and egg. Shape into 1-inch meatballs. Place on rack in roasting pan. Bake 15 minutes or until cooked.

2. In large saucepan, combine meatballs and spaghetti sauce. Cook until heated through. Serve over cooked pasta.

Makes 6 to 8 servings

Prep Time: 10 minutes • **Cook Time:** 20 minutes

Tip

To easily make evenly-shaped meatballs, pat meat mixture on waxed paper into 8×6×1-inch rectangle. With knife, cut crosswise and lengthwise into 1-inch rows. Roll each small square into a ball.

Turkey and Macaroni

1 teaspoon vegetable oil
1½ pounds ground turkey
2 cans (10¾ ounces each) condensed tomato soup, undiluted
1 can (16 ounces) corn, drained
½ cup chopped onion
1 can (4 ounces) sliced mushrooms, drained
2 tablespoons ketchup
1 tablespoon mustard
   Salt and black pepper
2 cups uncooked macaroni, cooked and drained

Slow Cooker Directions

1. Heat oil in large nonstick skillet over medium-high heat. Brown turkey, stirring to break up meat. Transfer turkey to slow cooker.

2. Add soup, corn, onion, mushrooms, ketchup, mustard, salt and pepper to slow cooker; mix well. Cover; cook on LOW 6 to 8 hours or on HIGH 3 to 4 hours.

3. Stir in macaroni. Cover; cook on LOW 30 minutes.

Makes 4 to 6 servings

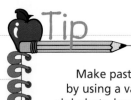

Tip

Make pasta dishes more fun by using a variety of shapes like alphabets, bows, wheels, spirals and shells. Be sure to adjust the cooking time for each type of pasta to avoid overcooking.

String Cheese
Spaghetti & Meatballs

1 pound ground beef
½ cup Italian seasoned dry bread crumbs
1 egg
1 jar (1 pound 10 ounces) RAGÚ® Organic Pasta Sauce
1 cup cubed mozzarella cheese (about 4 ounces)
8 ounces regular or whole wheat spaghetti, cooked and drained

In medium bowl, combine ground beef, bread crumbs and egg; shape into 12 meatballs.

In 3-quart saucepan, bring Pasta Sauce to a boil over medium-high heat. Gently stir in uncooked meatballs.

Reduce heat to low and simmer covered, stirring occasionally, 20 minutes or until meatballs are done. To serve, toss meatballs and sauce with mozzarella cheese and hot spaghetti.

Makes 4 servings

Prep Time: 20 minutes • **Cook Time:** 20 minutes

Tip

Kids love spaghetti. To prepare this recipe in a rush, purchase frozen fully-cooked meatballs. Heat according to package directions with the pasta sauce. Toss with the cheese and spaghetti. This dish will be done in half the time.

Sausage Vegetable Rotini Soup

6 ounces bulk sausage
1 cup chopped yellow onion
1 cup chopped green bell pepper
3 cups water
1 can (about 14 ounces) diced tomatoes
¼ cup ketchup
2 teaspoons beef bouillon granules
2 teaspoons chili powder
4 ounces uncooked tri-colored rotini pasta
1 cup frozen corn, thawed

1. Spray Dutch oven with nonstick cooking spray; heat over medium-high heat. Add sausage; cook 3 minutes or until no longer pink, breaking up sausage into small pieces. Add onion and pepper; cook 3 to 4 minutes or until onion is translucent.

2. Add water, tomatoes, ketchup, bouillon granules and chili powder; bring to a boil over high heat.

3. Stir in pasta and return to a boil. Reduce heat to medium-low and simmer, uncovered, 12 minutes. Stir in corn and cook 2 minutes. *Makes 4 servings*

Tip

When packing school lunches, don't forget to add a packet of hand wipes to clean hands before they touch the food. Also include a colorful napkin and the appropriate eating utensils.

Finger-Lickin' Chicken Salad

½ **cup diced roasted skinless chicken**
½ **stalk celery, cut into 1-inch pieces**
¼ **cup drained mandarin orange segments**
¼ **cup red seedless grapes**
 2 **tablespoons lemon yogurt**
 1 **tablespoon mayonnaise**
¼ **teaspoon soy sauce**
⅛ **teaspoon pumpkin pie spice or cinnamon**

1. Toss together chicken, celery, oranges and grapes in plastic container; cover.

2. For dipping sauce, combine yogurt, mayonnaise, soy sauce and pumpkin pie spice in small bowl. Place in small plastic container; cover.

3. Pack chicken mixture and dipping sauce in insulated bag with ice pack. To serve, dip chicken mixture into dipping sauce.

Makes 1 serving

Peanut-Caramel Dip

¼ cup peanut butter
2 tablespoons caramel ice cream topping
2 tablespoons milk
1 large apple, thinly sliced
4 large pretzel rods, broken in half

1. Combine peanut butter, caramel topping and milk in small saucepan. Heat over low heat, stirring constantly, until mixture is melted and warm. Cool and divide evenly among small containers.

2. Serve dip with apple and pretzel rods.   *Makes 4 servings*

Microwave Directions: Combine all ingredients except apple and pretzel rods in small microwavable dish. Microwave on MEDIUM (50%) 1 minute; stir well. Microwave an additional minute or until mixture is melted.

Orange Yogurt Dip for Fresh Fruit

1 carton (8 ounces) low-fat plain yogurt
2 tablespoons honey
    Grated peel of ½ SUNKIST® orange
2 SUNKIST® oranges, peeled and segmented
1 medium unpeeled apple, sliced*
1 medium banana, peeled and cut into chunks*

*Sprinkle cut apple and banana with small amount of orange or lemon juice to prevent fruit from darkening.

In small bowl, combine yogurt, honey and orange peel. Serve as dip with oranges, apple and banana.   *Makes 4 servings*

Peanut-Caramel Dip

Dreamy Orange Cheesecake Dip

1 package (8 ounces) cream cheese, softened
½ cup orange marmalade
½ teaspoon vanilla
2 cups whole strawberries
2 cups cantaloupe chunks
2 cups apple slices

1. Combine cream cheese, marmalade and vanilla in small bowl; mix well.

2. Serve with fruit dippers.   *Makes 8 to 12 servings*

Note: This dip can be prepared ahead of time. Portion into small containers. Store, covered, in refrigerator for up to 2 days.

Watermelon Kebobs

6 ounces (1-inch cubes) fat free turkey breast
6 ounces (1-inch cubes) reduced fat Cheddar cheese
18 cubes (1-inch) seedless watermelon
6 (6-inch) bamboo skewers

Alternate cubes of watermelon between cubes of turkey and cheese threaded onto each skewer.   *Makes 6 servings*

Favorite recipe from *National Watermelon Promotion Board*

Bananas & Cheesecake Dipping Sauce

½ **cup sour cream**
2 **ounces cream cheese**
2 **tablespoons plus 1 teaspoon milk**
1 **packet sugar substitute** *or* **1 tablespoon sugar**
½ **teaspoon vanilla**
  Nutmeg (optional)
6 **medium yellow or red bananas, unpeeled**

1. Place all ingredients except bananas in blender; blend until smooth. Pour 2 tablespoons sauce into each of 6 small plastic containers; sprinkle with nutmeg, if desired. Cover tightly. Refrigerate until needed or place containers in small cooler with ice.

2. Partially peel banana and dip directly into sauce; continue to peel and dip. *Makes 6 servings*

Tropical Coconut Cream Dipping Sauce: **Substitute coconut extract for vanilla.**

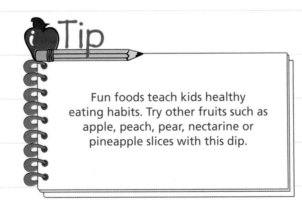

Tip

Fun foods teach kids healthy eating habits. Try other fruits such as apple, peach, pear, nectarine or pineapple slices with this dip.

Dilly Potato-Ham Salad To Go

8 small (about 8 ounces) red skin new potatoes, cut into quarters
¼ cup mayonnaise
2 tablespoons honey-Dijon salad dressing
1 tablespoon dill pickle relish
1 cup (4 ounces) chopped ham
½ cup shredded carrot
⅓ cup chopped zucchini or celery
2 tablespoons sliced green onion

1. Cook potatoes in small amount of salted boiling water in medium saucepan 10 to 15 minutes or until tender. Drain and cool.

2. Combine mayonnaise, salad dressing and pickle relish in small bowl. Add potatoes, ham, carrot, zucchini and onion. Gently toss until coated.

3. Pack in two plastic containers. Tightly cover and refrigerate for 2 to 24 hours. Pack containers in insulted lunch bag with ice packs.
Makes 2 to 4 servings

Peanut Butter Spread

½ cup part skim ricotta cheese
2 tablespoons peanut butter
1 tablespoon brown sugar
¼ teaspoon cinnamon
4 flour tortillas
1 sliced banana or apple, or jam

Mix ricotta cheese, peanut butter, brown sugar and cinnamon together. Spread over tortillas and cover with banana, apple or jam. Roll tortillas. Keep leftover spread refrigerated.
Makes 4 servings

Favorite recipe from **The Sugar Association, Inc.**

Fruit Salad with Orange Ginger Dressing

¼ **cup orange juice**
2 **tablespoons honey**
¼ **teaspoon ground ginger**
1 **can (20 ounces) DOLE® Pineapple Chunks, drained**
3 **cups watermelon, honeydew or cantaloupe chunks**
½ **cup blueberries**

• Stir together orange juice, honey and ginger in small bowl.

• Combine pineapple chunks, watermelon and blueberries in bowl. Pour dressing over salad. Toss to evenly coat. Cover; refrigerate 15 minutes to allow flavors to blend.

Makes 4 to 6 servings

Prep Time: 15 minutes • **Chill Time:** 15 minutes

Cucumber-Dill Dip

Salt
1 **cucumber, peeled, seeded and finely chopped**
6 **green onions, white parts only, chopped**
1 **package (3 ounces) cream cheese**
1 **cup plain yogurt**
2 **tablespoons fresh dill** *or* **1 tablespoon dried dill weed**
Carrot and celery sticks

1. Lightly salt cucumber in small bowl; toss. Refrigerate 1 hour. Drain cucumber; dry on paper towels. Return cucumbers to bowl and add onions. Set aside.

2. Place cream cheese, yogurt and dill in food processor or blender; process until smooth. Stir into cucumber mixture. Cover; refrigerate 1 hour. Spoon dip into individual plastic cups with lids. Pack with vegetables. *Makes about 2 cups dip*

Cherry Tomato Pops

4 strips string cheese sticks (1-ounce each)
8 cherry tomatoes
3 tablespoons ranch dressing

1. Slice string cheese in half lengthwise. Trim stem end of each cherry tomato and gently squeeze out about ¼ teaspoon of pulp and seeds.

2. Press end of string cheese into hollowed tomato to make cherry tomato pop. Serve with ranch dressing as dip.   *Makes 8 pops*

Cinnamon Apple Chips

2 cups unsweetened apple juice
1 cinnamon stick
2 Washington Red Delicious apples

1. In large skillet or saucepan, combine apple juice and cinnamon stick; bring to a low boil while preparing apples.

2. With paring knife, slice off ½ inch from tops and bottoms of apples and discard (or eat). Stand apples on either cut end; cut crosswise into ⅛-inch-thick slices, rotating apple as necessary to cut even slices.

3. Drop slices into boiling juice; cook 4 to 5 minutes or until slices appear translucent and lightly golden. Meanwhile, preheat oven to 250°F.

4. With slotted spatula, remove apple slices from juice and pat dry. Arrange slices on wire racks, making sure none overlap. Place racks on middle shelf in oven; bake 30 to 40 minutes until slices are lightly browned and almost dry to touch. Let chips cool on racks completely before storing in airtight container.

Makes about 40 chips

Tip: There is no need to core apples because boiling in juice for several minutes softens core and removes seeds.

Favorite recipe from **Washington Apple Commission**

Cream Cheese Dip with Vegetables

BLT Cukes

3 slices crisp-cooked bacon, chopped
½ cup finely chopped lettuce
½ cup finely chopped baby spinach
¼ cup diced tomato
1½ tablespoons mayonnaise
Pinch salt
¼ teaspoon black pepper
1 large cucumber

1. Combine bacon, lettuce, spinach and tomato with mayonnaise. Season with pepper; set aside.

2. Peel cucumber. Trim off ends and slice in half lengthwise. Use spoon to scoop out seeds; discard seeds. Divide BLT mixture between cucumber halves, mounding in hollowed areas. Cut into 2-inch pieces.   *Makes 8 to 10 pieces*

Note: Make these snacks when cucumbers are plentiful and large enough to easily hollow out with a spoon. You may make these up to 12 hours ahead of time and chill until serving.

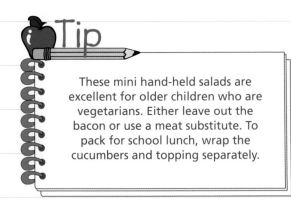

Tip

These mini hand-held salads are excellent for older children who are vegetarians. Either leave out the bacon or use a meat substitute. To pack for school lunch, wrap the cucumbers and topping separately.

Carrot, Walnut and Cranberry Slaw

2 cups shredded carrots*
¼ cup chopped walnuts
¼ cup dried sweetened cranberries
2 tablespoons mayonnaise
1 teaspoon lime juice
½ teaspoon honey
⅛ teaspoon salt
⅛ teaspoon black pepper

For convenience, use packaged shredded carrots; 2 cups is about half of a 10-ounce package.

1. Combine carrots, walnuts and cranberries in medium bowl. Combine mayonnaise, lime juice, honey, salt and pepper in small bowl. Stir mayonnaise into carrot mixture.

2. Pack individual servings into chilled wide-mouth vacuum container and include fork. Leftover carrot slaw can be refrigerated up to three days.   *Makes 4 servings*

Tuna 'n' Celery Sticks

4 ounces cream cheese, softened
3 tablespoons plain yogurt or mayonnaise
1½ teaspoons dried basil
1 (7-ounce) STARKIST Flavor Fresh Pouch® Tuna (Albacore or Chunk Light)
½ cup finely grated carrot or zucchini
½ cup finely shredded Cheddar cheese
2 teaspoons instant minced onion
10 to 12 celery stalks, cleaned and strings removed

In large bowl, mix together cream cheese, yogurt and basil until smooth. Add tuna, carrot, Cheddar cheese and onion; mix well. Spread mixture into celery stalks.   *Makes 5 to 10 servings*

Prep Time: 10 minutes

Citrus Zest Fruit Salad

1 can (20 ounces) DOLE® Pineapple Chunks, drained
2 cups seedless red grapes
1 green pear or red apple, cored, cubed
1 orange, peeled, diced
½ cup vanilla lowfat yogurt
1 teaspoon grated orange or lemon peel

• Combine pineapple chunks, grapes, pear and orange in medium bowl.

• Stir yogurt and orange peel into fruit mixture. Cover; refrigerate 15 minutes to allow flavors to blend. Garnish with orange curl and fresh mint, if desired. *Makes 4 to 6 servings*

Prep Time: 10 minutes • **Chill Time:** 15 minutes

Señor Nacho Dip

½ package (4 ounces) cream cheese, cubed
½ cup (2 ounces) shredded Cheddar cheese
¼ cup mild or medium chunky salsa
2 teaspoons milk
4 ounces tortilla chips or assorted fresh vegetable dippers

1. Combine cream cheese and Cheddar cheese in small saucepan; cook and stir over low heat until melted. Stir in salsa and milk; heat thoroughly, stirring occasionally. Cool completely.

2. Transfer dip to small containers. Pack with tortilla chips or vegetables. *Makes 4 servings*

Olé Dip: Substitute Monterey Jack cheese or taco cheese for Cheddar cheese.

Confetti Tuna in Celery Sticks

1 (3-ounce) STARKIST Flavor Fresh Pouch® Tuna (Albacore or Chunk Light)
½ cup shredded red or green cabbage
½ cup shredded carrots
¼ cup shredded yellow squash or zucchini
3 tablespoons reduced-calorie cream cheese, softened
1 tablespoon plain low-fat yogurt
½ teaspoon dried basil, crushed
Salt and pepper to taste
10 to 12 (4-inch) celery sticks, with leaves if desired

In a small bowl toss together tuna, cabbage, carrots and squash.

Stir in cream cheese, yogurt and basil. Add salt and pepper to taste.

With small spatula spread mixture evenly into celery sticks.

Makes 10 servings

Prep Time: 20 minutes

Tip

Choose fresh fruits instead of fruit juices when possible. Fresh fruit has more fiber and often less sugar than juices. If purchasing juices, select 100% juices. Be sure to read the labels to choose the most nutritious drinks.

Confetti Tuna in Celery Sticks

crunchy munchies

Spicy, Fruity Popcorn Mix

4 cups lightly salted popped popcorn
2 cups corn cereal squares
1½ cups dried pineapple wedges
1 package (6 ounces) dried fruit bits
   Butter-flavored nonstick cooking spray
2 tablespoons sugar
1 tablespoon ground cinnamon
1 cup yogurt-covered raisins

1. Preheat oven to 350°F.

2. Combine popcorn, cereal, pineapple and fruit bits in large bowl; mix lightly. Transfer to 15×10-inch jelly-roll pan. Spray mixture generously with cooking spray.

3. Combine sugar and cinnamon in small bowl. Sprinkle half of sugar mixture over popcorn mixture; toss lightly to coat. Spray mixture again with additional cooking spray. Add remaining sugar mixture; mix lightly.

4. Bake 10 minutes, stirring after 5 minutes. Cool completely in pan on wire rack. Add raisins; mix lightly.

Makes about 8½ cups snack mix

Brontosaurus Bites

4 cups air-popped popcorn
2 cups mini-dinosaur grahams
2 cups corn cereal squares
1½ cups dried apricots, diced
1 package (6 ounces) dried fruit bits
Butter-flavored nonstick cooking spray
1 tablespoon plus 1½ teaspoons sugar
1½ teaspoons ground cinnamon
½ teaspoon ground nutmeg
1 cup yogurt-covered raisins

1. Preheat oven to 350°F.

2. Combine popcorn, grahams, cereal, apricots and fruit bits in large bowl; mix lightly. Transfer to 15×10-inch jelly-roll pan. Spray mixture generously with cooking spray.

3. Combine sugar, cinnamon and nutmeg. Sprinkle half of sugar mixture over popcorn mixture; toss lightly to coat. Spray mixture again with additional cooking spray. Add remaining sugar mixture; mix lightly.

4. Bake snack mix 10 minutes, stirring after 5 minutes. Cool completely in pan on wire rack. Add raisins; mix lightly.

Makes 9 cups snack mix

Gorilla Grub: Substitute plain raisins for the yogurt-covered raisins and ¼ cup grated Parmesan cheese for the sugar, cinnamon and nutmeg.

Note: For school parties or take-home treats, wrap snack mix in festive colored paper napkins.

Brontosaurus Bites

Cinnamon Trail Mix

2 cups corn cereal squares
2 cups whole wheat cereal squares or whole wheat
 cereal squares with mini graham crackers
1½ cups oyster crackers
 ½ cup broken sesame snack sticks
 2 tablespoons butter, melted
 1 teaspoon ground cinnamon
 ¼ teaspoon ground nutmeg
 ½ cup bite-size fruit-flavored candy pieces

1. Preheat oven to 350°F. Spray 13×9-inch baking pan with nonstick cooking spray.

2. Place cereals, oyster crackers and sesame sticks in prepared pan; mix lightly.

3. Combine butter, cinnamon and nutmeg in small bowl; mix well. Drizzle evenly over cereal mixture; toss to coat.

4. Bake 12 to 14 minutes or until golden brown, stirring gently after 6 minutes. Cool completely. Stir in candies.

Makes 6 cups snack mix

Crispy Parmesan Pita Chips

2 (6-inch) rounds pita bread, split open
¼ cup butter, melted
3 tablespoons grated Parmesan cheese
1 teaspoon dried parsley flakes

1. Preheat oven to 375°F. Brush inside of pitas with butter.

2. Cut each circle into 8 wedges and place on 2 baking sheets. Combine cheese and parsley; sprinkle evenly over wedges. Bake 10 to 12 minutes or until light golden brown.

Makes 8 to 12 servings

Savory Pita Chips

2 rounds whole wheat or white pita bread
   Nonstick olive oil cooking spray
3 tablespoons grated Parmesan cheese
1 teaspoon dried basil
¼ teaspoon garlic powder

1. Preheat oven to 350°F. Line baking sheet with foil; set aside.

2. Carefully cut each pita around edges to form 2 rounds. Cut each round into 6 wedges.

3. Place wedges, rough side down, on prepared baking sheet; coat lightly with cooking spray. Turn wedges over; spray again.

4. Combine Parmesan cheese, basil and garlic powder in small bowl; sprinkle evenly over pita wedges.

5. Bake 12 to 14 minutes or until golden brown. Cool completely.

Makes 4 servings

Cinnamon Crisps: Substitute butter-flavored cooking spray for olive oil-flavored cooking spray, and 1 tablespoon sugar mixed with ¼ teaspoon ground cinnamon for Parmesan cheese, basil and garlic powder.

Tip

Pack pita chips with individual containers of Cucumber-Dill Dip on page 83 or Cream Cheese Dip on page 86.

Soft Pretzels

**1 package (16 ounces) hot roll mix plus ingredients
   to prepare mix**
1 egg white
2 teaspoons water
2 tablespoons *each* **assorted coatings: coarse salt, sesame
   seeds, poppy seeds, dried oregano**

1. Prepare hot roll mix according to package directions.

2. Preheat oven to 375°F. Spray baking sheets with nonstick cooking spray; set aside.

3. Divide dough equally into 16 pieces; roll each piece with hands to form rope, 7 to 10 inches long. Place on prepared cookie sheets; form into desired shape (hearts, wreaths, pretzels, snails, loops, etc.).

4. Beat egg white and water in small bowl until foamy. Brush onto dough shapes; sprinkle each shape with 1½ teaspoons of one coating.

5. Bake 15 minutes or until golden brown.   *Makes 16 servings*

Fruit Twists: Omit coatings. Prepare dough and roll into ropes as directed. Place ropes on lightly floured surface. Roll out, or pat, each rope into rectangle, ¼ inch thick; brush each rectangle with about 1 teaspoon spreadable fruit or preserves. Fold each rectangle lengthwise in half; twist into desired shape. Bake as directed.

Cheese Twists: Omit coatings. Prepare dough and roll into ropes as directed. Place ropes on lightly floured surface. Roll out, or pat, each rope into rectangle, ¼ inch thick. Sprinkle each rectangle with about 1 tablespoon shredded Cheddar or other flavor cheese. Fold each rectangle lengthwise in half; twist into desired shape. Bake as directed.

"M&M's"® Family Party Mix

2 tablespoons butter or margarine*
¼ cup honey*
2 cups favorite grain cereal or 3 cups granola
1 cup coarsely chopped nuts
1 cup thin pretzel pieces
1 cup raisins
2 cups "M&M's"® Chocolate Mini Baking Bits

*For a drier mix, eliminate butter and honey. Simply combine dry ingredients and do not bake.

Preheat oven to 300°F. In large saucepan over low heat, melt butter; add honey until well blended. Remove from heat and add cereal, nuts, pretzel pieces and raisins, stirring until all pieces are evenly coated. Spread mixture onto ungreased cookie sheet and bake about 10 minutes. Do not overbake. Spread mixture onto waxed paper and allow to cool completely. In large bowl combine mixture and "M&M's"® Chocolate Mini Baking Bits. Store in tightly covered container. *Makes about 6 cups snack mix*

Critter Munch

1½ cups animal cracker cookies
**½ (6-ounce) package Cheddar or original flavor
   goldfish-shaped crackers (1½ cups)**
1 cup dried tart cherries
1 cup candy-coated chocolate candy
1 cup honey-roasted peanuts

Put cookies, goldfish crackers, cherries, candy and peanuts in a large mixing bowl.

Carefully stir with a spoon.

Store in a tightly covered container at room temperature.

Makes 6 cups

Favorite recipe from **Cherry Marketing Institute**

Sweet Nothings Trail Mix

5 cups rice and corn cereal squares
1½ cups raisins
1½ cups small thin pretzel sticks, broken into pieces
1 cup candy-coated chocolate pieces
1 cup peanuts (optional)

1. Decorate small resealable food storage bags with favorite stickers, if desired.

2. Combine cereal, raisins, pretzels, chocolate pieces and peanuts, if desired, in large resealable food storage bag; shake well. Distribute evenly among decorated bags.

Makes 10 cups snack mix

Serve It With Style!: If you'd rather use this recipe as a party favor, wrap handfuls of trail mix in pink plastic wrap and tie with red, white or pink ribbons.

Prep and Cook Time: 10 minutes

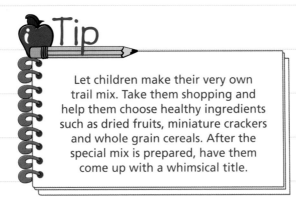

Tip

Let children make their very own trail mix. Take them shopping and help them choose healthy ingredients such as dried fruits, miniature crackers and whole grain cereals. After the special mix is prepared, have them come up with a whimsical title.

Rabbit Power Brownie Cupcakes

1¼ cups sugar

1 cup all-purpose flour

½ cup unsweetened cocoa powder

½ teaspoon baking soda

½ teaspoon baking powder

¼ teaspoon salt

½ cup baby carrots

⅔ cup vegetable oil

2 eggs

¼ cup milk

1 teaspoon vanilla

1 container (16 ounces) chocolate frosting

Colored sprinkles (optional)

1. Preheat oven to 350°F. Line 20 standard (2½-inch) muffin cups with paper baking cups.

2. Combine sugar, flour, cocoa, baking soda, baking powder and salt in large bowl. Place carrots in food processor; process using on/off pulsing action until finely chopped. Add carrots, oil, eggs, milk and vanilla to flour mixture. Beat with electric mixer at low speed until blended. Increase speed to medium. Beat 2 minutes. Spoon into muffin cups, filling about two-thirds full.

3. Bake 15 minutes or until toothpick inserted into centers comes out clean. Cool completely on wire racks. Frost cupcakes with chocolate frosting. Decorate with sprinkles.   *Makes 20 cupcakes*

Carrot Cream Cheese Cupcakes

1 package (8 ounces) cream cheese, softened
¼ cup powdered sugar
1 package (18¼ ounces) spice cake mix, plus ingredients
     to prepare mix
2 cups grated carrots
2 tablespoons finely chopped candied ginger (optional)
1 container (16 ounces) cream cheese frosting
3 tablespoons maple syrup

1. Preheat oven to 350°F. Line 14 jumbo (3½-inch) muffin cups with paper baking cups.

2. Beat cream cheese and powdered sugar in large bowl with electric mixer at medium speed 1 minute or until light and fluffy. Cover and refrigerate until needed.

3. Prepare cake mix according to package directions; stir in carrots and ginger, if desired.

4. Fill muffin cups one-third full (about ¼ cup batter). Place 1 tablespoon cream cheese mixture in center of each cup. Top with remaining batter (muffin cups should be two-thirds full).

5. Bake 25 to 28 minutes or until toothpicks inserted into centers come out clean. Cool in pans on wire racks 10 minutes. Remove cupcakes to racks; cool completely.

6. Mix frosting and maple syrup until well blended. Frost tops of cupcakes.   *Makes 14 cupcakes*

Buried Cherry Bars

1 jar (10 ounces) maraschino cherries
1 package (18¼ ounces) devil's food cake mix
   without **pudding in the mix**
1 cup (2 sticks) butter, melted
1 egg
½ teaspoon almond extract
1½ cups semisweet chocolate chips
¾ cup sweetened condensed milk
½ cup chopped pecans

1. Preheat oven to 350°F. Lightly grease 13×9-inch baking pan. Drain maraschino cherries, reserving 2 tablespoons juice. Cut cherries into quarters.

2. Combine cake mix, butter, egg and almond extract in large bowl; mix well. (Batter will be very thick.) Spread batter in prepared pan. Lightly press cherries into batter.

3. Combine chocolate chips and sweetened condensed milk in small saucepan. Cook over low heat, stirring constantly, until chocolate melts. Stir in reserved cherry juice. Spread chocolate mixture over cherries in pan; sprinkle with pecans.

4. Bake 35 minutes or until almost set in center. Cool completely in pan on wire rack. *Makes 24 bars*

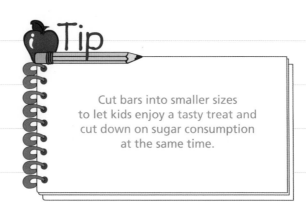

Tip

Cut bars into smaller sizes to let kids enjoy a tasty treat and cut down on sugar consumption at the same time.

Pumpkin Spiced and Iced Cookies

2¼ cups all-purpose flour
1½ teaspoons pumpkin pie spice
1 teaspoon baking powder
½ teaspoon baking soda
½ teaspoon salt
1 cup (2 sticks) butter or margarine, softened
1 cup granulated sugar
1 can (15 ounces) LIBBY'S® 100% Pure Pumpkin
2 large eggs
1 teaspoon vanilla extract
2 cups (12-ounce package) NESTLÉ® TOLL HOUSE®
   Semi-Sweet Chocolate Morsels
1 cup chopped walnuts (optional)
  Vanilla Glaze (recipe follows)

PREHEAT oven to 375°F. Grease baking sheets.

COMBINE flour, pumpkin pie spice, baking powder, baking soda and salt in medium bowl. Beat butter and granulated sugar in large mixer bowl until creamy. Beat in pumpkin, eggs and vanilla extract. Gradually beat in flour mixture. Stir in morsels and nuts. Drop by rounded tablespoon onto prepared baking sheets.

BAKE for 15 to 20 minutes or until edges are lightly browned. Cool on baking sheets for 2 minutes; remove to wire racks to cool completely. Spread or drizzle with Vanilla Glaze.

Makes about 5½ dozen cookies

Vanilla Glaze: **COMBINE** 1 cup powdered sugar, 1 to 1½ tablespoons milk and ½ teaspoon vanilla extract in small bowl; mix well.

Crispy Cocoa Bars

¼ **cup (½ stick) margarine**
¼ **cup HERSHEY'S Cocoa**
5 cups miniature marshmallows
5 cups crisp rice cereal

1. Spray 13×9×2-inch pan with vegetable cooking spray.

2. Melt margarine in large saucepan over low heat; stir in cocoa and marshmallows. Cook over low heat, stirring constantly, until marshmallows are melted and mixture is smooth and well blended. Continue cooking 1 minute, stirring constantly. Remove from heat.

3. Add cereal; stir until coated. Lightly spray spatula with vegetable cooking spray; press mixture into prepared pan. Cool completely. Cut into bars.   *Makes 24 bars*

Granola Raisin Bars

1 package (18¼ ounces) yellow cake mix with
   pudding in the mix, divided
½ **cup (1 stick) butter, melted, divided**
1 egg
4 cups granola cereal with raisins

1. Preheat oven to 350°F. Lightly spray 13×9-inch baking pan with nonstick cooking spray. Reserve ½ cup cake mix; set aside.

2. Combine remaining cake mix, 4 tablespoons melted butter and egg in large bowl; stir until well blended. (Dough will be thick and sticky.) Spoon dough into prepared pan. Cover with plastic wrap and press dough evenly into pan, using plastic wrap to keep hands from sticking to dough.

3. Bake 8 minutes. Meanwhile, combine reserved cake mix, granola cereal and remaining 4 tablespoons melted butter in medium bowl; stir until well blended. Spread mixture evenly over partially baked bars.

4. Return pan to oven; bake 15 to 20 minutes or until edges are lightly browned. Cool completely.   *Makes 15 to 20 bars*

Peanut Butter Chips and Jelly Bars

1½ cups all-purpose flour
½ cup sugar
¾ teaspoon baking powder
½ cup (1 stick) cold butter or margarine
1 egg, beaten
¾ cup grape jelly
1⅔ cups (10-ounce package) REESE'S® Peanut Butter Chips, divided

1. Heat oven to 375°F. Grease 9-inch square baking pan.

2. Stir together flour, sugar and baking powder in large bowl. With pastry blender or two knives, cut in butter until mixture resembles coarse crumbs. Add egg; blend well. Reserve 1 cup mixture; press remaining mixture onto bottom of prepared pan. Stir jelly to soften; spread evenly over crust. Sprinkle 1 cup peanut butter chips over jelly. Stir together reserved crumb mixture with remaining ⅔ cup chips; sprinkle over top.

3. Bake 25 to 30 minutes or until lightly browned. Cool completely in pan on wire rack. Cut into bars. *Makes about 16 bars*

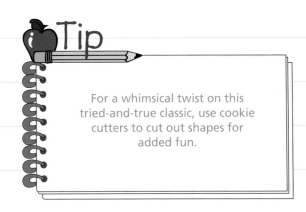

Tip

For a whimsical twist on this tried-and-true classic, use cookie cutters to cut out shapes for added fun.

Cookies & Cream Cupcakes

2¼ cups all-purpose flour
1 tablespoon baking powder
½ teaspoon salt
1⅔ cups sugar
1 cup milk
½ cup (1 stick) butter, softened
2 teaspoons vanilla
3 egg whites
1 cup crushed chocolate sandwich cookies (about 10 cookies)
plus additional for garnish
1 container (16 ounces) vanilla frosting

1. Preheat oven to 350°F. Lightly grease 24 standard (2½-inch) muffin cups or line with paper baking cups.

2. Sift flour, baking powder and salt together in large bowl. Stir in sugar. Add milk, butter and vanilla; beat with electric mixer at low speed 30 seconds. Beat at medium speed 2 minutes. Add egg whites; beat 2 minutes. Stir in 1 cup crushed cookies.

3. Spoon batter evenly into prepared muffin cups, filling two-thirds full. Bake 20 to 25 minutes or until toothpick inserted into centers comes out clean. Cool in pans on wire racks 10 minutes. Remove cupcakes to racks; cool completely.

4. Frost cupcakes; garnish with additional crushed cookies.

Makes 24 cupcakes

Note: To reduce sugar consumption, do not frost cakes and cookies. Frostings often just stick to the plastic wrap. Many cookies and cakes are very delicious without the extra sugar topping.

Original Nestlé® Toll House®
Chocolate Chip Cookies

2¼ cups all-purpose flour
1 teaspoon baking soda
1 teaspoon salt
1 cup (2 sticks) butter or margarine, softened
¾ cup granulated sugar
¾ cup packed brown sugar
1 teaspoon vanilla extract
2 large eggs
2 cups (12-ounce package) NESTLÉ® TOLL HOUSE®
Semi-Sweet Chocolate Morsels
1 cup chopped nuts

PREHEAT oven to 375°F.

COMBINE flour, baking soda and salt in small bowl. Beat butter, granulated sugar, brown sugar and vanilla extract in large mixer bowl until creamy. Add eggs, one at a time, beating well after each addition. Gradually beat in flour mixture. Stir in morsels and nuts. Drop by rounded tablespoon onto ungreased baking sheets.

BAKE for 9 to 11 minutes or until golden brown. Cool on baking sheets for 2 minutes; remove to wire racks to cool completely.

Makes about 5 dozen cookies

Pan Cookie Variation: **GREASE** 15×10-inch jelly-roll pan. Prepare dough as above. Spread in prepared pan. Bake for 20 to 25 minutes or until golden brown. Cool in pan on wire rack. Makes 4 dozen bars.

Mini Doughnut Cupcakes

1 cup sugar
1½ teaspoons ground cinnamon
1 package (18¼ ounces) yellow or white cake mix,
   plus ingredients to prepare mix
1 tablespoon ground nutmeg

1. Preheat oven to 350°F. Grease and flour 24 mini (1¾-inch) muffin cups. Combine sugar and cinnamon in small bowl; set aside.

2. Prepare cake mix according to package directions; stir nutmeg into batter. Fill prepared muffin cups two-thirds full.

3. Bake about 12 minutes or until lightly browned and toothpick inserted into centers comes out clean.

4. Remove cupcakes from pans; roll in sugar mixture until completely coated. Serve warm or at room temperature.

Makes about 48 cupcakes

Note: **Save any remaining cinnamon-sugar mixture to sprinkle on toast and pancakes.**

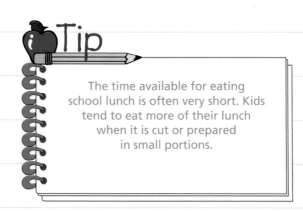

Tip

The time available for eating school lunch is often very short. Kids tend to eat more of their lunch when it is cut or prepared in small portions.

Acknowledgments

The publisher would like to thank the companies and organizations listed below for the use of their recipes and photographs in this publication.

Cherry Marketing Association

Chilean Fresh Fruit Association

Delmarva Poultry Industry, Inc.

Dole Food Company, Inc.

The Golden Grain Company®

The Hershey Company

The Hidden Valley® Food Products Company

Hillshire Farm®

Hormel Foods, LLC

Jennie-O Turkey Store®

© Mars, Incorporated 2006

National Turkey Federation

National Watermelon Promotion Board

Nestlé USA

Reckitt Benckiser Inc.

Sargento® Foods Inc.

StarKist® Seafood Company

The Sugar Association, Inc.

Reprinted with permission of Sunkist Growers, Inc.
All Rights Reserved.

Unilever

Washington Apple Commission

Index

Metric Conversion Chart

VOLUME MEASUREMENTS (dry)

1/8 teaspoon = 0.5 mL
1/4 teaspoon = 1 mL
1/2 teaspoon = 2 mL
3/4 teaspoon = 4 mL
1 teaspoon = 5 mL
1 tablespoon = 15 mL
2 tablespoons = 30 mL
1/4 cup = 60 mL
1/3 cup = 75 mL
1/2 cup = 125 mL
2/3 cup = 150 mL
3/4 cup = 175 mL
1 cup = 250 mL
2 cups = 1 pint = 500 mL
3 cups = 750 mL
4 cups = 1 quart = 1 L

VOLUME MEASUREMENTS (fluid)

1 fluid ounce (2 tablespoons) = 30 mL
4 fluid ounces (1/2 cup) = 125 mL
8 fluid ounces (1 cup) = 250 mL
12 fluid ounces (1 1/2 cups) = 375 mL
16 fluid ounces (2 cups) = 500 mL

WEIGHTS (mass)

1/2 ounce = 15 g
1 ounce = 30 g
3 ounces = 90 g
4 ounces = 120 g
8 ounces = 225 g
10 ounces = 285 g
12 ounces = 360 g
16 ounces = 1 pound = 450 g

DIMENSIONS

1/16 inch = 2 mm
1/8 inch = 3 mm
1/4 inch = 6 mm
1/2 inch = 1.5 cm
3/4 inch = 2 cm
1 inch = 2.5 cm

OVEN TEMPERATURES

250°F = 120°C
275°F = 140°C
300°F = 150°C
325°F = 160°C
350°F = 180°C
375°F = 190°C
400°F = 200°C
425°F = 220°C
450°F = 230°C

BAKING PAN SIZES

Utensil	Size in Inches/Quarts	Metric Volume	Size in Centimeters
Baking or Cake Pan (square or rectangular)	8×8×2	2 L	20×20×5
	9×9×2	2.5 L	23×23×5
	12×8×2	3 L	30×20×5
	13×9×2	3.5 L	33×23×5
Loaf Pan	8×4×3	1.5 L	20×10×7
	9×5×3	2 L	23×13×7
Round Layer Cake Pan	8×1½	1.2 L	20×4
	9×1½	1.5 L	23×4
Pie Plate	8×1¼	750 mL	20×3
	9×1¼	1 L	23×3
Baking Dish or Casserole	1 quart	1 L	—
	1½ quart	1.5 L	—
	2 quart	2 L	—